BASEBALL LEGENDS

Hank Aaron
Grover Cleveland Alexander
Ernie Banks
Johnny Bench
Yogi Berra
Roy Campanella
Roberto Clemente
Ty Cobb
Dizzy Dean
Joe DiMaggio
Bob Feller
Jimmie Foxx
Lou Gehrig
Bob Gibson
Rogers Hornsby
Walter Johnson
Sandy Koufax
Mickey Mantle
Christy Mathewson
Willie Mays
Stan Musial
Satchel Paige
Brooks Robinson
Frank Robinson
Jackie Robinson
Babe Ruth
Duke Snider
Warren Spahn
Willie Stargell
Honus Wagner
Ted Williams
Carl Yastrzemski
Cy Young

CHELSEA HOUSE PUBLISHERS

BOB FELLER

Morris Eckhouse

Introduction by
Jim Murray

Senior Consultant
Earl Weaver

CHELSEA HOUSE PUBLISHERS
New York • Philadelphia

Produced by James Charlton Associates
New York, New York.

Designed by Hudson Studio
Ossining, New York.

Typesetting by LinoGraphics
New York, New York.

Picture research by Jenny McGregor
Cover illustration by Dan O'Leary

First Printing

1 3 5 7 9 8 6 4 2

Library of Congress Cataloging-in-Publication Data

Eckhouse, Morris
    Bob Feller/Morris Eckhouse; introduction by Jim Murray.
        p. cm.—(Baseball Legends)
    Includes bibliographical references.
    Summary: Follows the life of the baseball player from its beginning
to his retirement years.
    ISBN 0-7910-1174-7
    ISBN 0-7910-1208-5 (pbk.)
    1. Feller, Bob, 1918-   —Juvenile literature. 2. Baseball
players—United States—
Biography—Juvenile literature.
[1. Feller, Bob, 1919-   . 2. Baseball players.] I. Title.   II. Series.
GV865.F4E25   1990
92—dc20
[796.357'092]
[B]

CONTENTS

WHAT MAKES A STAR

Jim Murray

No one has ever been able to explain to me the mysterious alchemy that makes one man a .350 hitter and another player, more or less identical in physical makeup, hard put to hit .200. You look at an Al Kaline, who played with the Detroit Tigers from 1953 to 1974. He was pale, stringy, almost poetic-looking. He always seemed to be struggling against a bad case of mononucleosis. But with a bat in his hands, he was King Kong. During his career, he hit 399 home runs, rapped out 3,007 hits, and compiled a .297 batting average.

Form isn't the reason. The first time anybody saw Roberto Clemente step into the batter's box for the Pittsburgh Pirates, the best guess was that Clemente would be back in Double A ball in a week. He had one foot in the bucket and held his bat at an awkward angle—he looked as though he couldn't hit an outside pitch. A lot of other ballplayers may have had a better-looking stance. Yet they never led the National League in hitting in four different years, the way Clemente did.

Not every ballplayer is born with the ability to hit a curveball. Nor is exceptional hand-eye coordination the key to heavy hitting. Big-league locker rooms are filled with players who have all the attributes, save one: discipline. Every baseball man can tell you a story about a pitcher who throws a ball faster than anyone has ever seen but who has no control on or *off* the field.

The Hall of Fame is full of people who transformed themselves into great ballplayers by working at the sport, by studying the game, and making sacrifices. They're overachievers—and winners. If you want to find them, just watch the World Series. Or simply read about New York Yankee great Lou Gehrig; Ted Williams, "the Splendid Splinter" of the Boston Red Sox; or the Dodgers' strikeout king Sandy Koufax.

A pitcher *should* be able to win a lot of ballgames with a 98-miles-per-hour fastball. But what about the pitcher who wins 20 games a year with a fastball so slow that you can catch it with your teeth? Bob Feller of the Cleveland Indians got into the Hall of Fame with a blazing fastball that glowed in the dark. National League star Grover Cleveland Alexander got there with a pitch that took considerably longer to reach the plate; but when it did arrive, the pitch was exactly where Alexander wanted it to be— and the last place the batter expected it to be.

There are probably more players with exceptional ability who didn't make it to the major leagues than there are who did. A number of great hitters, bored with fielding practice, had to be dropped from their team because their home-run production didn't make up for their lapses in the field. And then there are players like Brooks Robinson of the Baltimore Orioles, who made himself into a human vacuum cleaner at third base because he knew that working hard to become an expert fielder would win him a job in the big leagues.

A star is not something that flashes through the sky. That's a comet. Or a meteor. A star is something you can steer ships by. It stays in place and gives off a steady glow; it is fixed, permanent. A star works at being a star.

And that's how you tell a star in baseball. He shows up night after night and takes pride in how brightly he shines. He's Willie Mays running so hard his hat keeps falling off; Ty Cobb sliding to stretch a single into a double; Lou Gehrig, after being fooled in his first two at-bats, belting the next pitch off the light tower because he's taken the time to study the pitcher. Stars never take themselves for granted. That's why they're stars.

STRAIGHT TO THE MAJORS

On July 6, 1936, 17-year-old Bob Feller received the chance of a lifetime. Although he was already considered a brilliant pitching prospect by the Cleveland Indians, who had just signed him, the young righthander was still scheduled for the minor leagues.

Feller was headed for Cleveland's minor-league club at Fargo, North Dakota. But first, the Indians had an exhibition game to play with the St. Louis Cardinals. General manager Cy Slapnicka, the man who had signed Feller to pitch for Cleveland, decided to see what his prospect could do against the Cards.

The Cardinals were nicknamed the "Gashouse Gang" because of the players' rowdy, high-spirited playing style. The colorful 1936 Cards included future Hall of Famers Johnny Mize, Joe Medwick, player-manager Frankie Frisch, and pitcher Dizzy Dean. As a boy in Van Meter, Iowa, Bobby Feller had followed the exploits of these Cardinals. Now, he would face these legends, trying to show that he belonged in the major leagues with them.

Young Bob Feller signed his first professional contract before he graduated from high school.

9

Player-coach George Uhle worked the first three innings against St. Louis, and then it was Bob's turn. As the nervous youngster took the mound in the fourth inning, manager Steve O'Neill, a great catcher in his playing days, went behind the plate.

Brusie Ogrodowski was the first major-league batter to face Bob Feller and witness the 17-year-old's blazing fastball up close. After one fast strike and a faster pitch inside, Ogrodowski bunted meekly for an out.

At the time, many people considered Bob to be effectively wild. Although the young pitcher would sometimes experience control problems, the fear batters had of his erratic fastball could also be a great advantage. According to baseball legend, Frisch took one look at the wild right-hander and removed himself from the lineup.

Feisty shortstop Leo Durocher was the next batter to challenge Bob Feller. He waved at three Feller fastballs to become Feller's first major-league strikeout victim. Durocher showed a healthy respect for Bob's blazing speed and suspect control. After the second strike, the story goes, he ran to the dugout and hid behind the water cooler. "You can't hit me from here," he joked.

But Feller was not laughing. He was all business as he struck out Art Garibaldi to retire the side.

Bob's second inning proved that major-league pitching was not quite as easy as he had made it look against the first three batters. After a strikeout, Terry Moore singled and Stu Martin walked. Now Feller was really in trouble. The high leg-kick he used to help generate his pitching power was a definite disadvantage when there were men on base. As he wound up both baserunners took off. Bob's fastball sailed off O'Neill's mitt, allowing Moore to score and Stu Martin to reach third.

The veteran Cardinals saw no need to risk being injured by a Feller fastball and did not dig in at the plate. Both Pepper Martin and Rip Collins struck out to end Bob's second inning.

By his third inning, Bob was beginning to feel confident. His blazing fastball struck out the side. In three innings, Bob Feller had faced 12 batters, allowed two hits, one walk, and one run, and got eight of nine outs on strikes.

After the game, a photographer asked Dizzy Dean if he would pose with Feller for a picture. "It's all right with me," Dean said, "but you'd better ask him if it's okay with him." Of course, Bob was thrilled to pose with the legendary St. Louis hurler.

Feller had impressed everybody with his performance against the Cardinals. There would be no detour to the minor leagues for him. Just 17 years old, Bob Feller was ready for the majors.

Robert William Andrew Feller was born to Bill and Margaret Feller on November 3, 1918, in Van Meter, Iowa. Although farming was Bill Feller's life's work, he had once been a semi-pro ballplayer, and he passed his love of the game on to his son.

Little Bobby Feller had plenty of room to develop his athletic skills on the Feller farm. As a young boy, he would throw stones and corn cobs into the stream that ran through the farm. And still later, of course, he would fire a baseball into the strike zone.

Bob's desire to become a baseball player was strong. He was always asking his father to play catch, and Bill Feller was happy to oblige. In addition to giving the boy lots of pointers, the senior Feller came up with a highly effective conditioning program for him. Farming was very physical work. By carrying hay and water, milking cows, and performing other essential chores, Bob would quickly develop the back, leg, and arm muscles needed to throw a big-league fastball. His mother, a schoolteacher and registered

The 10-year-old Bob Feller in uniform on his family's farm in Van Meter, Iowa.

nurse, also helped with nutritious meals and an early-to-bed, early-to-rise schedule.

When Bob was nine years old he went to see an exhibition game in Des Moines featuring baseball greats Babe Ruth and Lou Gehrig. He was anxious to get a baseball autographed by the two superstars, but the price was five dollars, a considerable sum in the 1920s. The enterprising Feller quickly raised the money, though, by bagging 50 gophers. The county treasurer was offering 10 cents for each gopher caught. Bob's bounty was exactly enough to get the autographed baseball.

The following year, his father brought home a fielding glove and catcher's mitt, a uniform, a bat, spikes, and a big supply of baseballs. Then he put up lights in the backyard so he and Bob would have more practice time. Bill Feller was determined to give his son every opportunity to become a big-leaguer.

Seventeen-year-old Bob Feller (sitting third from right) with his Oakview team in 1936.

By 1931, at age twelve, Bob was playing for the Adel, Iowa, American Legion team. During one stretch, he pitched five no-hitters in seven games for Adel. Although Bob was covering third base and shortstop as well as pitching, it was clear his future was on the mound. Father and son felt that Bob should concentrate on his pitching. By then, Bill Feller and his 12-year-old pitching protégé were a hot topic in Van Meter. Bill decided to showcase the young pitching talent by building him his own baseball field on the farm, something his own father had done for him when he was a boy. Bob and Bill cleared and leveled the land, fenced in the diamond with chicken wire, put up seats and a scoreboard, and named it Oakview Park. They charged fans 35 cents to watch young athletes from Van Meter and the surrounding area play there. Oakview Park was an important step in the baseball development of Bob Feller, a field of dreams that would soon become reality.

When Bob Feller began playing American Legion baseball in Des Moines, he easily adapted to the tougher competition and helped his West Des Moines team win the state championship in the annual tournament.

In 1935, 16-year-old Bob Feller began pitching for the Farmers' Union Insurance team, a semi-pro club in Des Moines. Cy Slapnicka, himself an Iowa native, was on his way to scout a local pitcher named Claude Passeau when he decided to stop off and check out another young pitcher he'd heard about—Robert Feller. And when Slapnicka saw Bob Feller, he forgot about Claude Passeau. He went straight to the Feller farm and offered Bob a contract to play professional baseball.

Feller pitching against the Washington Senators.

The agreement guaranteed Bob $500 if he was retained on the Fargo roster at the end of the '36 baseball season. The contract also stipulated that Bob could visit his parents, or they could visit him, during the season. With his father acting as legal guardian, Bob Feller accepted one dollar to validate the contract and become a member of the Fargo baseball club, a minor-league affiliate of the Cleveland Indians.

Bob Feller never did pitch for Fargo, though. A sore arm prevented the 17-year-old from pitching for anybody during the early part of 1936. He finally reported to Cleveland in June, after his high-school class was dismissed for the summer. Returning to sandlot action, Bob pitched for the Cleveland Rosenblums, a local amateur team. On June 26th, he pitched five innings against the Lorain (Ohio) Grilles, allowing just one hit with nine strikeouts. On July 1, Bob recorded 16 strikeouts while defeating the Akron Atlantic Foundries, 3–2. That performance convinced the Indians management to send their prospect up against St. Louis. After the game on July 6, Alex Zirin, a Cleveland *Plain Dealer* sportswriter raved, "Seldom before has a Cleveland-owned pitcher shown such blazing speed as the youngster, who pitches for the Rosenblums in Class A, fired past the dodging Cards yesterday."

Cleveland baseball fans had been waiting for a championship club since 1920. One look at Bob Feller told them that he could help put the Indians back on top.

Exhibition heroics aside, young Bob Feller

was brought along slowly by the Indians. His first appearance in a regular-season major-league game was in Washington, DC's Griffith Stadium on July 19, 1936. Used in a mop-up role, with Cleveland trailing 8–2, Feller was typically wild. He hit Red Kress in the ribs. Four more misguided pitches sent Monte Weaver walking to first before Ben Chapman grounded out. The next batter, Buddy Lewis, was Feller's first strikeout victim in a regular season game. But because record keeping was not very efficient in those days, Feller never received official credit for striking him out.

After five more appearances in mostly one-sided games, Feller got his first big-league start against the St. Louis Browns. Although the Browns would lose 95 games in 1936, their lineup included such stars as Jim Bottomley, Beau Bell, and Lyn Lary. The Indians, well behind the first-place Yankees, were willing to give their young fireballer a start.

After a shaky beginning, Feller settled down and showed off the powerful fastball that had brought him to Cleveland. After five scoreless innings, Bob had 10 strikeouts. He finally allowed one run in the sixth, but the Indians came back with three. Despite the August heat, he finished up with three more shutout innings and five more strikeouts. In his very first start, Bob Feller had jumped into the record books. No pitcher in American League history ever struck out more batters in his starting debut. Feller also became the youngest hurler to start, complete, and win a major-league game.

Feller's next two outings proved just how tough the big leagues could be. Boston's Fenway Park was the scene of the rookie's second start but this time he was wild and almost always behind in the count. Allowing five runs in five innings, he suffered his first defeat.

Feller's next stop was Yankee Stadium in New York, and there things got worse. Feller struck out the Yankees' leadoff batter, Frank Crosetti, but walked the next three men up. He then allowed 3 hits and gave up 5 runs before being lifted.

Having experienced the best and the worst of times, Feller settled down for some solid pitching. He struck out 10 and won his second game against the Browns on Labor Day. The following Sunday, he went against the last-place Philadelphia Athletics. Putting aside some experiments he had tried with off-speed pitches, the young phenom was at his fastest. That meant an embarrassing 9 walks but an impressive 17 strikeouts. The performance earned Feller another line in the record books: only Dizzy Dean had struck out as many batters in one modern (since 1901) major-league game. With two more wins in his final three starts, Feller closed out the season with a respectable 5-3 record in 14 games.

Bob Feller's future looked bright indeed. But for the present, Bob had a serious problem to deal with. As it turned out, the 1935 contract Bob had signed to pitch professionally was not entirely legal. Though Cy Slapnicka represented the Fargo club, he was also representing the Cleveland Indians. Because baseball rules at the time stipulated that a major-league club could not sign a sandlot player, some clubs bent the rules by signing young prospects like Feller to minor-league contracts, then moving them directly to the majors.

At the end of the '36 season Lee Keyser, owner of the Des Moines club of the Western League, protested Feller's signing to Judge Kenesaw Mountain Landis, Commissioner of Baseball. Landis conducted a thorough investigation of the signing, including an interview with Bob and his father. When the commissioner asked Bob if he was happy in Cleveland, Bob said he was. With the best interests of the young pitcher in mind, Landis ruled that Feller would remain with the Indians. He did fine Cleveland $7,500, however, to be paid to the Des Moines club.

Although $7,500 was a lot of money in those days, it was nothing compared to what Bob Feller could have gotten out of the situation. Until the 1970s, a reserve clause bound a player for life to the club that signed him. Only an illegal signing or mistake could make a previously signed player a free agent, eligible to go to the highest bidder. Had Bob asked for, and been granted, the option to become a free agent, there were teams ready to pay him $100,000 just to

Bob Feller signs his contract in 1936 as Cy Slapnicka (left) and Bill Feller look on.

sign. This was a high figure in the mid-1930s, when $20,000 was considered a great salary. Despite the dollar figures being thrown around, the Fellers had given their word that Bob would pitch for Cleveland, and that is exactly what Bob Feller intended to do. He willingly signed a $10,000 contract, with no bonus, to pitch for the Indians in 1937.

No sooner was one crisis settled than another arose. After being chosen to start the second game of the 1937 season, against St. Louis, Feller threw a curveball in the first inning and immediately felt a pop in his arm. Relying on his fastball, he went on to strike out 11 batters in six innings before reporting the injury to manager O'Neill. Angry that Bob had not told him immediately and worried that there might be permanent damage, O'Neill then removed Feller from the game.

As the manager feared, the soreness remained and kept Bob inactive. Rest was prescribed, and the young pitcher went home to take final exams and attend his high-school graduation. But rest did not seem to be helping. Several specialists were unable to provide a cure. Finally, Bob was taken to a chiropractor just around the corner from Cleveland's League Park. Dr. Austin felt the damaged right arm and promptly diagnosed a dislocated ulna, the bone on the little-finger side of Bob's forearm. Grabbing Bob's right wrist and elbow, the doctor gave the arm a powerful twist and popped the bone right back into place. And with that, Feller was as good as new.

Bob celebrated the 4th of July by pitching four innings in a loss to the Detroit Tigers. His next start, a week later, was also against the

Tigers. This time, he pitched a complete game but lost again. In both games, wildness was the problem. Although he gave up just one hit in the first game and two in the second, Feller walked 10 batters altogether and lost each game by one run.

Despite a 0-3 record, Feller eagerly faced the New York Yankees in huge Cleveland Municipal Stadium the following Sunday. The biggest crowd of the season was on hand to see him battle Red Ruffing to a 1–1 tie after eight innings. Then the Yankees loaded the bases in the ninth for their young slugger, Joe DiMaggio. Getting two quick strikes, Bob received the signal for a curve from catcher Frank Pytlak. Feller unloosed the pitch, DiMaggio hit a long, grand-slam home run, and New York defeated Cleveland 5–1.

Feller rebounded from his 0-4 start with four wins in his next six decisions, including a 16-strikeout performance against the Red Sox, before facing the Yankees again in early September. For seven innings, Feller threw his hardest and held New York scoreless. Then DiMaggio hit another homer, but this time Feller went the distance for a 4–2 win, with 12 strikeouts. Gehrig, fighting for the American League batting championship, struck out three times. By going the full route against the mighty Yankees, Bob Feller made it clear that he was ready to handle the toughest batters around.

Feller finished out the season with 9 wins in his final 12 decisions and a remarkable 150 strikeouts in 149 innings pitched. Only veterans Lefty Gomez, Bobo Newsom, and Lefty Grove had more strikeouts than Bob in 1937, and none came close to his average of more than one strikeout per inning pitched.

3

RAPID ROBERT—BASEBALL'S FASTEST PITCHER

A fearsome sight for a batter was the high kick and powerful motion of Rapid Robert. On September 13, 1936, Feller set a modern American-League record with 17 strikeouts against the Athletics.

In 1938, Bob Feller had, along with a new manager, a renewed goal of becoming a top major-league pitcher. But for all of his great natural talent, Feller was still more of a thrower than a pitcher. Along with his 150 strikeouts in 1937 were 116 hits and 106 walks. Once a batter became a base runner, he was often able to steal bases because of Feller's high leg-kick and long windup. Cleveland's new manager, Ossie Vitt, instructed his pitcher to use a shorter leg-kick when men were on base. Feller took Vitt's advice to heart. As Mel Harder, a pitching teammate of Feller, later recalled, "He had that high kick and when he started kicking, runners just took off. Nobody stopped at first base. Bob went out to the rightfield wall at League Park. He didn't need a catcher, he'd throw continuously against that wall like he had a man on base. He kept working to where all he had to do was bend that knee a little and still get that momentum into his pitches."

Although his new pitch was not as fast as the old one, Feller knew that the change was necessary. Soon he was equally effective with or without baserunners.

Feller was on the mound for Cleveland's second game of the season against the St. Louis Browns. For five innings the Browns were hitless before Billy Sullivan took advantage of Feller's powerful motion, which threw him toward first base, by bunting toward third. Feller fielded the bunt, but his throw to first was late. It was the only hit the Browns could manage against Feller as he threw his first major-league shutout, a 9–0 win.

Feller quickly became the workhorse of the Cleveland pitching staff. More often than not, he would finish what he started. He pitched 9 or more innings in 20 of the 36 games he started. Unfortunately, wildness continued to plague him. He allowed 208 walks in 1938, a modern major-league record, 70 more than the American League mark set by Detroit's George Mullin in 1905.

But even the walks could not keep Rapid Robert from becoming a consistent winner. By July he was 9-2 with 94 strikeouts, the most in either league.

It was not surprising that Feller was chosen to join the greatest major leaguers at the annual All-Star Game, but things started to fall apart when he returned to Cleveland. Johnny Allen, 11-1 at mid season, hurt his arm when he slipped in a bathtub during the All-Star break, and won just three more games the rest of the season. And although Feller continued to rack up strikeouts, wins came less easily. From July 1 to September 1 he had a disappointing 3-7 record.

When Feller speculated that he might have

Bill Feller talking to his son Bob.

"lost" his fastball, the self-doubt made headlines in the Cleveland newspapers. It was then that Bill Feller came to the rescue with a much-needed pep talk and some good fatherly advice.

The 19-year-old hurler responded with 10 strikeouts and a complete-game win against the Athletics. However, against the Yankees on August 26, Feller suffered one of his worst losses. Allowing 9 walks, 15 hits, and 15 runs, he was charged with an embarrassing 15–9 defeat.

But Feller settled down and delivered another late-season surge as the Indians rallied for their best finish since 1926. With five wins in September for the second straight year, Feller tied Mel Harder as the team's top pitcher.

In his final appearance of 1938, Feller faced Hank Greenberg, the Tigers' slugging first baseman. Greenberg had already blasted 58 home runs and was looking to beat Babe Ruth's record of 60 home runs in one season. But it was Feller who stole the show. Fanning Greenberg twice, Bob had 12 strikeouts after five innings. Greenberg doubled in the sixth and scored one of two Detroit runs, but Feller struck out Chet Laabs for the third time and finished the frame with 14 strikeouts. When Laabs struck out again in the eighth, Feller was one strikeout away from tying his own record. After a strikeout and a single, Greenberg advanced to the plate. This time the big slugger flied out, leaving Feller one chance for a new record. He gave up his seventh walk, and then Laabs came to bat. Getting two strikes, Feller went once more to his blazing fastball. As Laabs watched it go by, umpire Cal Hubbard signaled strike three. Bob Feller had a new major-league record: 18 strikeouts in one game.

But Feller saw plenty of room for improvement. "Imagine walking the pitcher there in the eighth. And look how many guys I had two strikes on and didn't get." Nevertheless, Feller got enough strikeouts to edge out Bobo Newsom for his first strikout championship.

The improvement shown by Bob Feller and the Indians left both with high hopes for 1939. Twenty-year-old Bob Feller started his first Opening Day assignment and came through with 10 strikeouts and a 3-hit, 5–1 win against the Detroit Tigers.

Always tough in April, Feller finished the month with three complete-game wins and no losses. Then, on June 27, he faced the Tigers again in the first night game ever at Cleveland Municipal Stadium. Hitting the Feller fastball in daylight was tough enough, but facing Rapid Robert under the night lights was too much. Ex-Indian Earl Averill, now a Tiger, got his team's only hit, a sixth-inning single. A season-high 13 strikeouts accompanied the third one-hitter of Feller's career.

By mid-July, Feller was 14-3 and off to another All-Star Game. In the mid-summer classic, the American Leaguers 3–1 lead was threatened in the sixth inning when the Nationals loaded the bases. With one out and Pittsburgh's Arky Vaughan coming up, manager Joe McCarthy called Feller in from the bullpen. While 62,000 fans held their breath, a Feller fastball was hit right to second baseman Joe Gordon, who helped turn it into an inning-ending double play. Feller then pitched three more scoreless innings to preserve the 3–1 win for the American Leaguers.

Although Bob Feller kept on winning during the second half of the season, the rest of the Indians went on the warpath only against each other. They quickly dropped down in the standings as serious differences developed between several of the players and manager Ossie Vitt. Pytlak was unhappy that Rollie Hemsley had become Feller's "personal" catcher. Things got so bad that it was rumored the Indians would change managers. Instead, the big change came when shortstop Lou Boudreau and second baseman Ray Mack were called up from the minor leagues.

Back-to-back wins by Feller and Harder in a double-header against the Yankees, plus the addition of the two new players sparked a fast finish that placed the Indians in third place with an 87-67 record.

The largest number of those wins were credited to Feller. For the first time, he led the league's pitchers, with a 24-9 record. About all Feller was missing now was the elusive pennant.

4

A NEW DECADE

When Opening Day 1940 rolled around, the Cleveland players were still having troubles with their manager. For a moment, however, Bob Feller made all those problems disappear with the greatest pitching performance of his young career. On a blustery cold day at Comiskey Park in Chicago, Feller was hotter than ever. He walked five and struck out eight in a tight duel with White Sox pitcher Eddie Smith. Smith was almost as tough against Cleveland, giving up just a solo run.

With only one out separating Feller from a no-hitter, Taffy Wright came to the plate. Wright hit a hard grounder toward right field. But second baseman Mack made a spectacular play to nip the runner.

Bob Feller had pitched the first Opening Day

Feller receives the congratulations of his teammates on April 16, 1940, after pitching the only Opening Day no-hitter in major-league history. Left to right are: coach Luke Sewell, Johnny Humphries, Tom Wilson, Joe Dobson, Russ Peters, manager Oscar Vitt, George Martin, and Alva Bradley, president of the Indians.

no-hitter in major-league history. But he was quick to acknowledge that he had help. "Mack came up with two as sweet plays as I've ever seen," said Feller. "He was off balance when he scooped up Rosenthal's roller in the eighth, and how his throw ever beat Larry to the bag, I don't know. And I don't know how he ever knocked down Wright's smash in the ninth, to say nothing of retrieving the ball and throwing the guy out."

Although Feller lost two of his next three decisions, he then came up with six straight wins to lead the streaking Indians. But then he suffered back-to-back losses at New York and Boston, and the ever-critical Vitt berated his ace hurler. "How am I supposed to win with pitching like this?" the manager moaned.

That was the last straw for many of the Indians. Feller, Harder, and several other veterans went to see club owner Alva Bradley and asked him to change managers. Although the owner promised to investigate the situation, he refused to take any immediate action. Before the meeting ended, Bradley also asked his players to keep their discontent to themselves. That proved to be impossible, however, as Cleveland sportswriter Gordon Cobbledick got word from someone and broke the story. Almost instantly, the Indians were labeled "the Crybabies."

Meanwhile, the rival Yankees were having problems of their own, leaving Cleveland and Detroit to battle for first place throughout the season. At the All-Star break Feller was 13-5, good enough for another invitation to the dream game. But Feller's All-Star appearance was not very dramatic; he pitched the final two innings of a 4–0 A.L. loss, striking out three batters and allowing one run.

Vitt remained manager and the Cleveland players resolved to do the best they could, regardless of their personal feelings. By mid-August, Feller already had 20 wins and had reached the 200-strikeout mark for the third consecutive season. He was going the distance almost every time he started and was also pitching well in relief. Even when he was re-moved for a pinch-hitter in a game against Boston, Feller got his win. Down 5-2, the Indi-ans suddenly rallied with seven more runs to give Feller his 22nd victory and themselves a 4½ game lead over the Tigers. At Chicago, on September 1, the Indians broke a 4-4 tie with three runs in the ninth before Feller came in in relief to preserve the victory that kept Cleveland 3½ games ahead of the Tigers and the suddenly charging Yankees.

While most of the league found Bob Feller almost unbeatable, the one team that did man-age to beat him was Detroit. Of his 11 losses in 1940, 5 came at the hands of the Tigers. Detroit started a three-game sweep of Cleveland on September 4. The Indians had lost seven straight games and seen their once-solid lead dwindle away before Feller emerged from the bullpen again for an extra-inning victory.

Cleveland and Detroit remained neck and neck until their next meeting two weeks later. With Harder pitching, the Indians were ahead 4–1 after seven innings. But then the Tigers put two runners on base in the eighth. Vitt held a five-minute meeting at the mound before calling Feller in from the bullpen. Feller had just pitched two complete games in four days and was sched-uled to start two days later. Detroit quickly ambushed the exhausted hurler, with three consecutive singles off him. Vitt then removed Feller, but the damage had been done. Before the uprising finally ended, Detroit scored five times and held on for a 6–5 win—and a one-game lead over the Indians. The Tigers increased their edge in the next game, but then Feller kept his team's hopes alive with a much-needed 10–5 win, his 27th season victory.

When the two teams met again for the final three games of the year, Detroit had a commanding lead of two full games. With Feller starting, Detroit manager Del Baker reasoned that the Indians would probably win. Rather than waste one of his best pitchers in a losing battle, Baker took his chances with a rookie named Floyd Giebell, who had just been called up from Buffalo.

The Cleveland batters were in a terrible slump, and Giebell managed to avoid serious trouble in the early innings. Feller was having

Feller shows his pitching release and follow through.

control problems, but had given up no hits. In the fourth inning, however, Tiger Rudy York came to the plate with Charlie Gehringer on first. York hit a high fly down the left-field line, the shortest home-run distance in mammoth Municipal Stadium, and the ball landed three rows deep in the seats for a two-run homer. Although Feller allowed just one other hit, Giebell responded with the only shutout of his brief big-league career. Detroit's 2–0 win eliminated the Indians from the pennant race.

Despite their disappointing finish, the 1940 Indians were the winningest Cleveland club in almost two decades, and that was largely thanks to Bob Feller. Rapid Robert had turned in his best season yet and accounted for almost one-third of Cleveland's 89 triumphs.

Feller was also responsible for drawing record numbers of fans to the ballpark. As American League president William Harridge put it, "Whenever he appears, the attendance goes up.

That isn't true of any other individual in the game. It hasn't been true of anybody since [Babe] Ruth's time."

But even though Feller's fan appeal would later make him baseball's highest paid player, he would gladly have traded all of his individual honors for one team championship.

When the 1941 season dawned, baseball was not the only thing on Bob Feller's mind. Bill Feller had taken ill and was found to be suffering from cancer. On a happier note, the pitcher met and began courting his future wife, Virginia Winther.

While the Indians finished a distant fourth in 1941, little of the blame could be handed to Bob Feller. For the third straight year he led the league in innings pitched and games won. He also captured his fourth consecutive league strikeout crown. And to top it all off, Feller was honored with his first starting assignment in the All-Star Game. This time he contributed three scoreless innings to the American League's 7–5 victory.

At a still tender 22 years of age, Bob Feller already ranked with the greatest pitchers in baseball history. But then at the peak of his career, he put baseball heroics aside to serve his country in a much more important struggle.

On December 9, 1941, two days after Japanese bombers had attacked the United States military base at Pearl Harbor in Hawaii, Bob Feller joined the U.S. Navy. Even though he was entering the peak athletic years, Feller's patriotism outweighed even his love of baseball. Before going off to war, though, Feller had made sure his family would be secure by building them a new house and providing his ailing father and

Bob Feller (right) with Sam Chapman of the Philadelphia Athletics in Norfolk, Virginia, in early 1942 after both players had enlisted in the Navy.

his young sister with enough money for their needs.

Soon after his induction, which was broadcast nationally on the radio, Feller requested a transfer to gunnery school. By Christmas 1942, Bob was serving on the battleship U.S.S. *Alabama*, in charge of a 24-man anti-aircraft crew. The *Alabama* saw extensive duty in the Pacific Ocean, and for the next few years, the battle of professional baseball would be replaced with real life-and-death struggles.

Two other monumental events affected Feller during the war years. His father died in January 1943, just before Bob and Virginia were to be married. They decided that Bill Feller would have wanted them to proceed, and the wedding took place as planned. The Fellers would later have three sons: Stephen, born in 1945; Martin, born in 1947; and Bruce, born in 1950.

In April 1945, Feller was released from the *Alabama* and named manager of the Great Lakes naval baseball team in Illinois. Feller had played little baseball since joining the Navy, and his new assignment would provide a tune-up for a return to the majors. Amateur baseball also gave him a chance to play simply for fun again. Finally, after 44 months of military service, on August 21, 1945, Bob Feller was discharged from the Navy.

A big civic reception welcomed Feller home to Cleveland. No one was happier to have him back than Lou Boudreau, player-manager of the Indians since 1942. At the reception, Boudreau said, "This is the first time in history that a manager is so happy to have a pitcher back that he gave him his warm-up ball seven hours before game time." And with that, Boudreau

Feller cheers on his Great Lakes teammates in April, 1945 in a game against nearby Northwestern University.

pulled a baseball from his pocket and presented it to Feller to the cheers of the crowd.

There was even more cheering at Municipal Stadium on August 24, when almost 50,000 fans came out to see Feller face his old rivals, the Detroit Tigers. When he entered the Navy, Feller was without a doubt the most dominant pitcher in baseball. Feller pitched before the Cy Young Award was established to honor the best pitcher in baseball in each year. Seeking to properly honor those active before the award was instituted in 1956 the Society for American Baseball Research (SABR) conducted a poll to choose retroactive Cy Young winners. Bob Feller was SABR's Cy Young choice for 1939, 1940, and 1941.

His prewar ability could not be questioned. But as he faced the first Tiger batter, everyone wondered if he could be the same after almost four years away from professional baseball.

They did not have to wonder long. Opposing Feller on the mound was Hal Newhouser, the American League's Most Valuable Player in 1944 and 1945, the only pitcher ever to win the award in consecutive years. Newhouser was also pitching for a championship contender, while the Indians were also-rans. But Detroit managed just four hits. Rapid Robert set 12 Tigers down with strikeouts in recording his first win of the season.

Feller made just nine appearances in 1945, finishing up his abbreviated season with a 5-3 record, identical to his rookie mark in 1936. Now, just as then, the Cleveland hurler still had much to prove. And, once again, he would quickly prove himself one of baseball's all-time greats.

5

THE SUPER SEASONS

By 1946, the Cleveland Indians had gone more than a quarter of a century without winning a league championship. Their only pennant had come in 1920. But big changes were in store for the city on Lake Erie. One of the best of those changes would include the full-time return of Bob Feller.

At age 27, Feller was in the physical prime of his life. Strong and durable, he set out to reclaim his spot as baseball's top pitcher. He got off to a good start on Opening Day with a three-hitter and 10 strikeouts to defeat the White Sox 1–0. After losing two tough decisions, Feller and the Indians made their first Eastern road trip of the year. On April 30th at Yankee Stadium, Feller showed just how far he'd really come.

The New York Yankees were a virtual all-star team, the acid test for any pitcher. But it was a test that Feller passed with flying colors. For eight innings he kept the Yanks' big bats silent. But New York pitcher Bill Bevens was also tough. He held the Indians scoreless until the ninth inning, when catcher Frankie Hayes hit a

Feller pitches against Joe DiMaggio in Yankee Stadium.

solo home run. In the bottom of the inning, New York's leadoff batter, Snuffy Stirnweiss, was safe on an error. Then Henrich sacrificed the runner to second. DiMaggio worked the count to three-and-two, then grounded to short as the runner took third. Feller still hadn't given up a hit when Charlie Keller came to bat. "King Kong" Keller was an imposing batter, but Feller was overpowering. Keller hit a weak grounder to second baseman Ray Mack, and Mack threw to Fleming for the final out of Bob Feller's second no-hitter.

"I think it was the best game I have ever pitched," Feller said. "I threw a lot of fastballs and sliders and I'm glad that's what I did," the jubilant pitcher explained. "I don't mind admitting I was a little peeved entering the game about stories that I couldn't throw hard anymore. Before the game I made up my mind that I would throw harder than I ever did before."

Feller had made his point. And in the process he made a true believer out of Joe DiMaggio. "Any pitcher who had as much on the ball as he did today deserved a no-hitter," the Yankee slugger admitted. "Fast? Well, he only threw me two curveballs all day and those were wide in the ninth. He looks as great, or greater, than ever to me."

With that no-hitter behind him, Feller really caught fire, winning 14 of his next 17 decisions. In his second All-Star Game start, he again blanked the Nationals for three innings, and he was credited with the Americans' 12–0 victory, By the end of July, he had already won 20 games and was racking up strikeouts at a record-setting pace.

Record keeping had been steadily upgraded

Feller with Negro-League great Satchel Paige during their barnstorming tour in 1946. Paige shut out Feller's team in one game, and two years later, in July 1948, he was signed by the Indians. He was 6-1 during his first season.

since the early days of baseball, but many contradictions still existed in the 1940s. The accepted major-league strikeout record was 343 by Rube Waddell of the Philadelphia Athletics in 1904. That was the mark Bob Feller was after in '46. As the Indians visited Detroit on the final weekend of the season, Feller had 25 wins but was still 6 short of Waddell's strikeout mark.

Coming out of the bullpen in the first game, he fanned 6 batters to bring his season's total to 343. Then in the final game of the year, he struck out another 5 while defeating Detroit 4–1. His total of 348 strikeouts was recognized as the major-league single-season record. Later research indicated that Waddell may have had

349 strikeouts in 1904, but for the moment Feller was the acknowledged strikeout king. (Both he and Waddell would eventually be surpassed by Sandy Koufax and Nolan Ryan.)

Bob Feller finished his first full season since 1941 right back where he belonged—on top. He earned his sixth strikeout title, led the league in games pitched, games started, complete games, innings pitched, shutouts, and, for the fourth time, games won (26).

Rapid Robert had by now become the highest paid player in baseball. He gave the game his best, and fully expected the kind of compensation a top professional would earn for any job.

But Feller found time for fun, too. In an article for *Sport* magazine, Hal Lebovitz described Feller as "a passionate and dedicated practical joker." Using fireworks, dancing ties, phony newspaper headlines, and whatever other gadgets he could obtain, Feller kept his friends

A happy Cleveland president Bill Veeck is "held up" in January 1948 by Feller. Feller signed a contract for more than $80,000 making him the highest-paid player in baseball.

and acquaintances on their toes. According to Lebovitz, one of Feller's favorite pranks was "to plant noisy but harmless bombs in the autos of guests partying at his home. Some explode under the hood when the car starts, others, connected to each tire, erupt periodically after the car is rolling along the highway." Virginia Feller attributed her husband's playful side to the serious business of baseball and the deadly nature of World War II. As she saw it, pranks provided a fun balance to the other aspect of his life.

There were high expectations in Cleveland when Bill Veeck purchased the Indians in 1946. Veeck was baseball's greatest promoter, while Feller was its biggest drawing card. And although the Indians had set a club record by drawing over one million fans in 1946, they'd once again fallen short of their goal—an A.L. championship.

For a while, it looked as if 1947 might finally be their year. After a disappointing Opening Day loss, Feller bounced back with three consecutive shutouts, including the ninth and tenth one-hitters of his career. But then disaster struck.

Against Philadelphia on June 13th, Rapid Robert fanned eight of nine batters in the first three innings. Pitching to Barney McCosky, he snapped off a curve and got number nine. It was a costly strikeout, though; for in the process Feller misstepped into a small rut in the pitching mound where he usually landed when throwing a fastball. He fell to the ground, injuring his knee as well as his pitching arm. Instead of leaving the game, he continued to pitch, working a total of eight innings and striking out 12.

On August 20, 1946 at Washington's Griffith Stadium, Feller's fastball was timed on an Army chronograph at 144 feet per second, or 98.6 miles per hour.

Bob's work ethic demanded that he continue to pitch despite his injury, but he decided to bypass the 1947 All-Star Game to rest his knee.

In regular games, the ailing Feller continued to win, finishing the season with a league-high 20 victories. Although his 196 strikeouts again led the American League, they didn't come close to his previous totals. Bob Feller would never again be a dominant strikeout pitcher.

By 1948, the Indians looked like legitimate pennant contenders once again—except, ironically, for Feller. For the first time since 1937, the cornerstone of the Cleveland pitching staff had a losing record at the All-Star break. Still, he was again selected to the A.L. squad. This time, it was Veeck who insisted that Feller sit out the game.

Feller's problems continued after the break, but fortunately for Cleveland, Bob Lemon and rookie phenom Gene Bearden were on hand to take up the slack. The two young pitchers posted win after win. Boudreau was also having a great season and Larry Doby, who in 1947 became the first black player in the American League, provided extra power at the plate.

The Indians were soon locked in a four-team race with the Red Sox, Athletics, and Yankees. They needed a boost—and they got one when Feller returned to form. From August 1st until the regular season ended, he won 9 of 12 decisions, including all six in the heated September stretch drive. An outstanding, three-hit victory against the Red Sox on September 22nd moved the Tribe into a first-place tie with Boston. Just one more win—against Detroit on the final day of the regular season—would give them the pennant. But it wasn't to be that easy. Against his old rival, Hal Newhouser, Feller was defeated 7–1. Although he played no part in the one-game playoff that finally gave the Indians their first pennant since 1920, there could be no doubt in anyone's mind that they'd never have gotten that far without Bob Feller's 19 wins.

Feller got another chance to shine on Opening Day of the World Series, and he was determined to make the most of it. But Johnny Sain of the Boston Braves was equally determined. After seven innings the game was still scoreless when Feller committed a cardinal sin by walking the leadoff batter. Pinch-runner Phil Masi advanced to second on a sacrifice. Feller and Boudreau then teamed up on their own secret pick-off play. On a prearranged signal, both men would begin counting. Boudreau would break to second base and Feller would throw without ever looking at the shortstop. The play went off exactly as planned, with Feller throwing a perfect strike to Boudreau. Masi was caught off guard, but unfortunately so was umpire Bill

Pitcher Bob Lemon consoles Feller after his 1-0 heartbreaking loss to the Braves. Lemon, a converted outfielder who was elected to the Hall of Fame in 1976, was in centerfield when Feller threw his 1946 no-hitter in Yankee Stadium.

Stewart. All photographs of the play indicate that Masi was picked off, but Stewart called the runner safe. A single then brought Masi home with the only run of the game, and Feller suffered a heartbreaking, two-hit defeat.

Cleveland won the next three games, and then Feller was back on the mound before a record-setting crowd of 86,288 fans at Cleveland Municipal Stadium. The fans were ready to celebrate a championship, but once more Feller failed to deliver. He was way off his form, allowing seven runs before Boudreau finally pulled him out. To make matters worse, the fans booed the veteran hurler unmercifully as he left the field. Many sportswriters were equally unkind. Red Smith wrote a scathing article in *The Sporting News*. After taking several shots at Feller's financial interests, Smith wrote, "Poets in the

crowd insisted that what they were watching was poetic justice." And John F. Carmichael wrote, "He failed. He failed himself and those 86,288 fans."

Although he was naturally disappointed with his own poor personal performance, Feller was delighted when his teammates went on to win game 6—and the World Series. And so Bob Feller wound up the 1948 season with his first world championship ring.

Feller was not only rewriting the record book, he was writing on his own. In his 1948 baseball instructional book, *How to Pitch*, he attributed his success both on and off the field largely to dedication and plain hard work. "I would throw until I had told myself I had thrown enough," he explained. According to Feller, "Ninety-nine percent of the pitchers haven't thrown enough. They need to work for it." And even his harshest critics admitted that Bob Feller practiced what he preached.

THE COMEBACK

The next two seasons were disappointing both for Feller and the Indians. Cleveland's offense tailed off, and he was no longer the overpowering pitcher who could win by himself. The combination meant only 15 wins for Feller in 1949 and 16 wins in 1950.

As the '51 season got under way, baseball's so-called experts concluded that Feller's pitching days were numbered. The Indians had a new manager in Al Lopez, who had been a fine catcher and would guide some of the greatest pitching staffs in major-league history.

In 1951, one of those great pitchers, in his third decade in the majors, was Bob Feller. Relying more on a slider than a fastball, he reeled off 10 wins in his first 11 games. Although his new style cut down his strikeout count (he fanned just 42 batters in 95 innings), it gave him a big boost in wins.

Sam Chapman (left) and Luke Easter (right) congratulate Feller after his no-hitter against the Tigers on July 1, 1951. Easter knocked in the only two runs in Cleveland's 2-1 win.

On July 1st, Feller made his first home appearance of the year, against the Tigers. Never better against his great rivals, the Indian ace set down the first nine batters he faced. "He just didn't look right," pitching coach Harder later recalled. When Feller came off the mound after the second inning, the coach asked him if he felt all right. "Yeah, I feel all right" Feller replied, "I just haven't got a thing."

In the fourth inning, two errors helped Detroit score without a hit, but over the next four frames only two Tigers reached base, both on walks. Feller still had not given up a hit. The Indians took a 2–1 lead in the eighth inning, and then with two out in the ninth, suddenly only Vic Wertz stood between Bob Feller and immortality. Working the count to 3 balls and 2 strikes, Feller threw Wertz a slider. The pitch broke across the inside corner for strike three. Feller had his third no-hitter. Only two other pitchers, Larry Corcoran and Cy Young, had ever thrown three no-hit games, and both of them did it in the 19th century. Cy Young himself commented on Feller's no-hitter saying, "I was glad he did it. He's good enough to have won 20 games a season even back in the 1890s, but only because he had smartened up. The boy was trying to overpower all those hitters. I told him he'd never get away with it in the long run...I told him to mix up his stuff more...don't show them your overhand fastball every time."

Feller closed out July with another milestone victory: By defeating the Senators Feller posted his 224th win with the Indians to become the winningest pitcher in the team's history. Pitching coach Mel Harder had won 223 games while pitching for Cleveland. With a 22-8 record Feller

Feller's 1951 Bowman baseball card.

wound up as the American League leader in wins for the sixth time. He also became, again, the Indians' highest-paid player, after having taken a pay cut following the 1948 season. Only the Tribe's second-place finish behind the Yankees put a damper on another great season for the 32-year-old hurler.

Feller's comeback was short-lived, however. The kind of breaks that had gone his way in 1951 all seemed to go against him in 1952. In an April outing against St. Louis, for example, Feller allowed just one hit, thereby extending his major-league record for one-hitters to 11. But that one hit was enough for St. Louis to win the game. Ironically, the winner was Bob Cain, the loser in Feller's 1951 no-hitter against Detroit.

Despite Feller's struggles, the Indians again battled it out with the Yankees for first place. In

When the Indians played at home, Feller, who had a pilot's license, often would fly his own plane from his home in Gates Mills, Ohio to a landing field near Municipal Stadium. In the plane he kept a folding scooter, which he rode to the ball park.

Cleveland's vast Municipal Stadium, built to attract the 1932 Olympics, became the exclusive home of the Indians in 1947. Before that, the Indians split their games between Municipal Stadium and the smaller League Park. 86, 288 fans, the largest crowd in major-league history, saw the Braves beat Feller in game 5 of the 1948 World Series in Municipal Stadium.

the closing weeks of the season, Lopez decided to use his top three pitchers—Lemon, Wynn, and Garcia—exclusively. Feller did not pitch at all down the stretch, and the Indians did not win the pennant.

Having lost confidence in Feller, Lopez used him just 25 times in 1953, mostly against non-contending teams. The decreased workload seemed to agree with Feller, however. His record improved from 9-13 to 10-7 and his E.R.A. decreased by more than one run per nine innings. But even though he won three complete-game victories in September the Indians finished a distant second to the Yankees.

By 1954, Bob had pitched more than 3,500 major-league innings. But even though his 20-win seasons were all in the past, he was still able to contribute in limited action. Used sparingly by Lopez, Feller kept up with a squad that would win more games than any other in American League history. The Yankees won 103 games, more than they had in any of the five previous seasons when they won pennants. But the Indians won 111 games and the pennant.

Feller's contribution was a splendid 13-3 record. Moreover, Bob also recorded his 2,500th strikeout along the way. Only Walter Johnson and Cy Young had struck out more major-league batters than Rapid Robert Feller. But best of all, Cleveland made it to the World Series.

The Indians were favored to beat the National League champion New York Giants, and Bob was slated to pitch the fourth game of the Series. But neither expectation was fulfilled. When the Giants shocked Cleveland by winning the first three games, Lopez decided to go with Bob Lemon, instead of Feller, in the fourth game. But even Lemon could not do the job, and the Giants won the championship in four straight games. Feller's last chance for a World Series win, one of the few and most cherished goals he had not achieved, was gone forever.

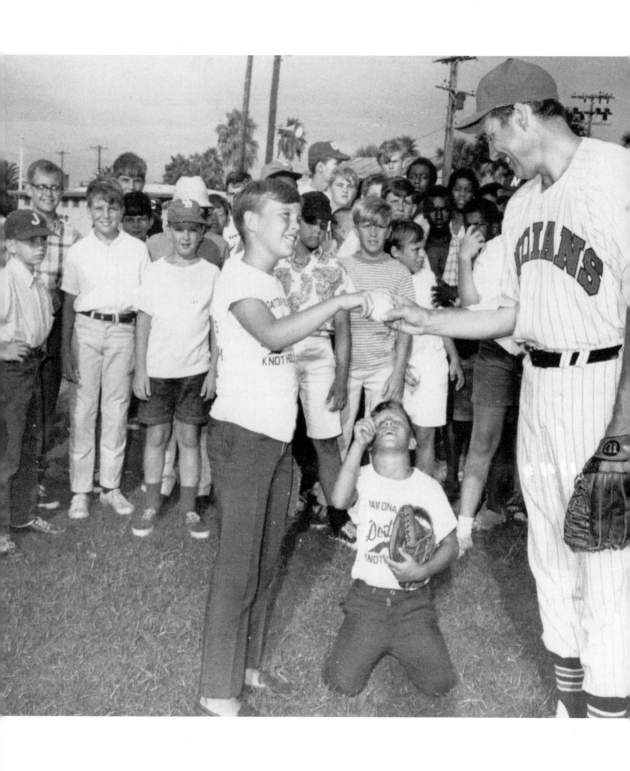

LIFE AFTER BASEBALL

A doubleheader against the Boston Red Sox on May 1, 1955, put the conclusion of Bob Feller's major-league pitching career in perspective. Feller won the first game, his 12th one-hitter, but he struck out just two batters along the way. The Indians won their other game as well—and in that one, rookie Herb Score struck out 16 batters. Although he was still managing to win some, the time was clearly coming for Feller to leave baseball to younger, stronger arms. Relegated to the bullpen by Lopez, Feller wound up with only four victories in 1955 and none in 1956. On September 9, 1956, the Indians staged Bob Feller Day at Cleveland Municipal Stadium to honor the winningest pitcher in the club's history.

Even as Feller was pitching less, he continued to give his all to the sport, becoming more and more involved in the behind-the-scenes business of baseball. When the Major League Baseball Players Association was formed in

Feller conducts one of a series of baseball clinics for Florida youngsters in 1969.

A model of the statue of Bob Feller to be erected in downtown Cleveland.

1953–54, Bob Feller was elected its first president. He was respected for his ability to combine business philosophy with the game of baseball. After retiring, he served on the Major League Players Pension committee, working to see that all players would be looked after when their professional careers ended.

Following the 1956 season, the Indians decided to give Feller his release. He could have gone to another team and padded out his already great statistical achievements. Instead, he decided to end his baseball career and to concentrate on his business as an insurance salesman. The Indians retired his uniform number 19, the first time in Tribe history a player was so honored.

In 1962, Bob Feller became eligible for induction into Baseball's Hall of Fame. To be voted in by members of the Baseball Writers Association of America, a player needed 75 percent of all the ballots cast. Feller was elected with a whopping 94 percent of the vote.

Other Hall of Famers welcomed Feller. Yankee great Joe DiMaggio called Feller "the best pitcher I ever hit against and without a doubt the best in the league." DiMaggio was not alone. Red Sox slugger Ted Williams admitted that Feller was his greatest test: "He was the best and I wanted to be the best, and three days before he pitched I would start thinking Robert Feller, Bob Feller."

Another honor came in 1969. As part of baseball's centennial celebration, Feller was named the greatest living right-handed pitcher in the majors.

Although there were highlights for baseball and Bob Feller in the 1960s, there were problems as well. Feller was finding that life away from professional baseball was difficult. His income had drastically decreased from his days as the highest paid player in the game, and his expenses outweighed his income. There were troubles at home, and Bob and Virginia were divorced in 1971. At one point, Feller sold a collection of his mementos to avoid having them confiscated in payment of his debts. Later, a lawsuit was necessary to reclaim the items, one of several legal actions he would be involved in. But Feller never was a quitter. He gradually paid his debts and regained stability. And in 1974 he married Anne Thorpe.

About the same time, there was a surge of interest in the collecting of baseball cards, artifacts, and memorabilia. Feller tirelessly traveled to sports collectors' shows signing autographs and promoting the game that had been so much a part of his life. Making appearances at old-timer's games and at minor-league ballparks, Bob was doing as much traveling as he had during his playing days.

And the honors continue. In 1988 the Cleveland Sports Legends Foundation chose Bob Feller to receive its first major honor, a 10-foot bronze statue to stand prominently in downtown Cleveland. The statue will be erected in the early 1990s. And so Rapid Robert Feller will always be remembered for his devotion to hard work, to his country, and to baseball.

CHRONOLOGY

Nov. 3,	1918	Born in Van Meter, Iowa
	1930	Begins playing American Legion baseball
	1935	Signs an agreement to pitch professionally
	1936	Strikes out eight St. Louis Cardinals while pitching for the Cleveland Indians in an exhibition game
	1936	Makes professional debut and becomes youngest pitcher to start, complete and win a major league game
	1937	Inactive much of season with mysterious arm ailment
	1938	Sets a major league record with 18 strikeouts against Detroit on October 2
Apr. 16,	1940	Becomes the first pitcher in major league history to throw an opening day no-hitter, vs. Chicago
Dec. 9,	1941	Joins U.S. Navy
	1945	Discharged from the Navy with eight battle stars
Apr. 30,	1946	Pitches second no-hitter, vs. New York Yankees
	1946	Sets major league season record with 348 strikeouts
	1947	Suffers arm injury, fastball never the same
	1948	Makes first World Series appearance, but loses twice, including a two-hit heartbreaker in the first game
	1951	Pitches third no-hitter, matching major league record, vs. Detroit
	1951	Becomes winningest pitcher in Cleveland Indians history
	1955	Pitches 12th one-hitter, setting a major league record, and becomes American League Player Representative
	1956	Retires from baseball at age 38
	1962	Elected to Baseball Hall of Fame, receiving 150 of a possible 160 votes
	1969	Chosen Greatest Living Righthanded Pitcher in Baseball

ROBERT WILLIAM ANDREW FELLER

CLEVELAND A.L. 1936 TO 1941
1945 TO 1956
PITCHED 3 NO-HIT GAMES IN A.L.,12 ONE HIT
GAMES. SET MODERN STRIKEOUT RECORD
WITH 18 IN GAME, 348 FOR SEASON. LED
A.L. IN VICTORIES 6 (ONE TIE) SEASONS.
LIFE TIME RECORD: WON 266, LOST 162,
P.C.,621, E.R. AVERAGE 3.25, STRUCKOUT 2581.

MAJOR LEAGUE STATISTICS

CLEVELAND INDIANS

YEAR	TEAM	W	L	PCT	ERA	G	GS	CG	IP	H	BB	SO	SHO
1936	CLE A	5	3	.625	3.34	14	8	5	62	52	47	76	0
1937		9	7	.563	3.39	26	19	9	148.2	116	106	150	0
1938		17	11	.607	4.08	39	36	20	277.2	225	208	240	2
1939		24	9	.727	2.85	39	35	24	296.2	227	142	246	4
1940		27	11	.711	2.61	43	37	31	320.1	245	118	261	4
1941		25	13	.658	3.15	44	40	28	343	284	194	260	6
1945		5	3	.625	2.50	9	9	7	72	50	35	59	1
1946		26	15	.634	2.18	48	42	36	371.1	277	153	348	10
1947		20	11	.645	2.68	42	37	20	299	230	127	196	5
1948		19	15	.559	3.56	44	38	18	280.1	255	116	164	3
1949		15	14	.517	3.75	36	28	15	211	198	84	108	0
1950		16	11	.593	3.43	35	34	16	247	230	103	119	3
1951		22	8	.733	3.50	33	32	16	249.2	239	95	111	4
1952		9	13	.409	4.74	30	30	11	191.2	219	83	81	1
1953		10	7	.588	3.59	25	25	10	175.2	163	60	60	1
1954		13	3	.813	3.09	19	19	9	140	127	39	59	1
1955		4	4	.500	3.47	25	11	2	83	71	31	25	1
1956		0	4	.000	4.97	19	4	2	58	63	23	18	0
Totals		266	162	.621	3.25	570	484	279	3827	3271	1764	2581	46
World Series (1 year)		0	2	.000	5.02	2	2	1	14.1	10	5	7	0
All-Star Games (5 years)		1	0	1.000	0.73	5	1	0	12.1	5	4	12	0

FURTHER READING

Allen, Lee and Tom Meany. *Kings of the Diamond*. New York: G.P. Putnam, 1965.

Brosnan, Jim. *Great Baseball Pitchers*. New York: Random House, 1965.

Devaney, John. *Baseball's Youngest Big Leaguers*. New York: Holt, Rinehart & Winston, 1969.

Feller, Bob. *How to Pitch*. New York: A.S. Barnes, 1948.

Feller, Bob with Bill Gilbert. *Now Pitching, Bob Feller*. New York: Birch Lane, 1990

Feller, Bob. *Pitching to Win*. New York: Grosset & Dunlap, 1952.

Feller, Bob. *Strikeout Story*. New York: A.S. Barnes, 1947.

Hirshberg, Al. *Greatest American Leaguers*. New York: G.P. Putnam, 1970.

Hollander, Zander. *Great American Athletes of the 20th Century*. New York: Random House, 1972.

Honig, Donald. *Baseball When the Grass Was Real*. New York: Coward, McCann, Geoghegan, 1975.

Meany, Tom. *Baseball's Greatest Players*. New York: Grosset & Dunlap, 1953.

Reidenbaugh, Lowell. *Cooperstown—Where Baseball's Legends Live Forever*. St. Louis, MO: The Sporting News Publishing Co, 1983.

Ritter, Lawrence and Donald Honig. *The 100 Greatest Baseball Players of All-Time*. New York: Crown, 1981.

Schoor, Gene. *Bob Feller—Hall of Fame Strikeout Star*. Garden City, NY: Doubleday, 1962.

INDEX

PICTURE CREDITS

AP/Wide World Photos: p. 44; Cleveland Indians: p. 52; Cleveland Sports Legends Foundation: p. 56; Cleveland Press Collection: pp. 12, 14, 42; National Baseball Library, Cooperstown, NY: pp. 2, 58, 60; Copyright The Topps Company, Inc.: p. 50; UPI/Bettmann Newsphotos: pp. 8, 16, 19, 22, 25, 28, 32, 33, 35, 36, 38, 41, 46, 48, 51, 54

MORRIS ECKHOUSE is executive director of the Cleveland Sports Legends Foundation and president of the Jack Graney Chapter of the Society for American Baseball Research (SABR). He is the author of two books, *Day-by-Day in Cleveland Indians History* and *Day-by-Day in Cleveland Browns History,* and co-author of *This Date in Pittsburgh Pirates History* and *Baseball's Milestone Season.* Born in Cleveland and raised in Shaker Heights, Ohio, he is a graduate of Ohio University and has contributed as a writer and researcher to a variety of publications. He lives with his wife Maria and son Allen Louis in South Euclid, Ohio.

JIM MURRAY, veteran sports columnist of the *Los Angeles Times*, is one of America's most acclaimed writers. He has been named "America's Best Sportswriter" by the National Association of Sportscasters and Sportswriters 14 times, was awarded the Red Smith Award, and was twice winner of the National Headliner Award. In addition, he was awarded the J. G. Taylor Spink Award in 1987 for "meritorious contributions to baseball writing." With this award came his 1988 induction into the National Baseball Hall of Fame in Cooperstown, New York.

EARL WEAVER is the winningest manager in Baltimore Orioles history by a wide margin. He compiled 1,480 victories in his 17 years at the helm. After managing eight different minor league teams, he was given the chance to lead the Orioles in 1968. Under his leadership the Orioles finished lower than second place in the American League East only four times in 17 years. One of only 12 managers in big league history to have managed in four or more World Series, Earl was named Manager of the Year in 1979. The popular Weaver had his number 5 retired in 1982, joining Brooks Robinson, Frank Robinson, and Jim Palmer, whose numbers were retired previously. Earl Weaver continues his association with the professional baseball scene by writing, broadcasting, and coaching.